THE ARCH AND ITS SHADOW

poems 1972 – 2007

Derek Sellen

GW00703518

First published in 2009
by Arch and its Shadow Press
5 Lime Kiln Road
Canterbury
Kent CT1 3QH

archanditsshadow@yahoo.com

A catalogue record for this book is available
from the British Library

ISBN 978-0-9561467-0-0

Printed by Creeds, Broadoak, Bridport, Dorset DT6 5NL

In the meantime,
keep on imagining
while the cortex lasts.
(1993)

Poems in this selection have previously been published in various magazines and anthologies, including Agenda, Apostrophe, Arts Council New Poetry, Arts Now, Connections, Equinox, Frogmore Papers, Hand Luggage Only, Iron, Mint Sauce (Cinnamon Press), Orbis, PEN New Poetry, PEN New Writing, Poetry Review, Poetry South East, The Scarpfoot Zone, South East Poetry 2000, South East Review, Statement for the Prosecution, The Sunday Telegraph, The Sunday Times

Poems included in the selection have been awarded prizes in The National Poetry Competition, Rhyme International, The Open University Poetry Competition, Frogmore Papers competition, Cheltenham Festival Poetry Competition and other national, local and international competitions

Acknowledgement:
To Amy Bryan, Nebraska, for front cover photograph, to Mike Iddon and Sara Wicks for inspiration from their art and words

To all those who have encouraged me to write and to publish, most especially Elaine

Foreword

Derek Sellen's poems communicate an insatiable relish for life. His endlessly inventive imagination is equally at home with myth, fable, incidents at work, Chinese idioms, human animals in paintings by Piero di Cosimo, a philosopher's statue with a fag-end stuffed up its marble nostril, or tourists eating ice-cream in an ancient Greek spa as their counterparts will envisage them in some post-nuclear future: 'The ruins / make romantic places. Here, they ate ice-cream'. Yet this poet is no easy daydreamer: the pleasures of imagination and sensuality are constantly shadowed in his poems by the knowledge of actual or imminent loss and danger, like the radioactive threat submerged in the bizarre spiky beauty celebrated in 'Dungeness', or the picnickers watching their country explode below them in 'The Trip to the Waterfall', or the sinister virus that 'settles with the swan on sunlit water' in 'The Time of Bird Flu'.

As that Yeatsian line suggests, Sellen often echoes other poets (Shakespeare, Keats, Lawrence, D.J.Enright all come to mind) but without ever sounding like their disciple or imitator. His poems find beauty, human drama and strangeness everywhere - in an impoverished 'Honey-Bucket Man' (= latrine cleaner) in an unnamed Asian country attacking pin-up photos of girls as 'filth', in Jan van Eyck's painting of the Lamb of God as 'a stocky Flemish sheep/ radiating gold', in an unwary tourist dragged dripping by the Mafia from the Roman baths in Sicily, or in the shade of E.M. Forster visiting the caves at Ajanta, Maharashtra 'blessed by the image of the Bodhisattva, peeling but golden, seen by reflected light/ as if it graced the dark of Plato's Cave' . Many of Sellen's best poems are inspired by art, sometimes directly as in the poems contemplating scenes by Uccello or Piero di Cosimo, sometimes obliquely as in the enchanting upside-down world of 'Fish' inspired by a painting by Sara Wicks, 'where rocks sway/ while sun/ lights the lagoon night and moon the sand-dune day'. Literature too excites Sellen's imagination, as much or more than visual art. Old stories are re-lived by contemporary men and women in their own messy lives, like 'Baxter and Clara' which revisits the characters of 'Sons and Lovers' as they might have lived today. Or new myths are born from current events, as in 'The Springs' where the floods of autumn 2000 create legends of new saints and miraculous births in a 'cool and watery religion' that fades by August to a damp mark in the meadow, or 'Britannia's Daughter 2003' where the personification of post-modern England moves uncomfortably from taking 'my tits out for Page Three' through illness to finding an 'ancient hardy mother' who gives her strength but not consolation. Or old myths are re-invented, like the hauntingly sexy 'Anubis' about a legend of St Christopher's abstinence, or the dark fable 'War' in which an archetypal mother (Eve after the Fall?) tries vainly to pacify her warring greedy children, the snake and the cockerel who 'suck her teats raw, one / with his dry gums, the other his horn beak.' And myths also come alive on motorways where 'a farmhouse with geranium-crowded sills/ is seen at speed as darkness streaked with blood' ('Motorway near Basel'), or museums where girls shown Cretan figurines 'give sly smiles / which show / they too have met, fox-red and naked in the dark / of cave-like rooms, serpents that come to be their slaves' ('The Fox-Red Goddesses'). These are poems that, splendidly, enable their readers to live up to Sellen's own Keatsian injunction to 'keep on imagining / while the cortex lasts'.

Jan Montefiore,

Canterbury 2007

CONTENTS

4. THE LOWER REGION

5. THE APPROACH OF DARKNESS

ONE

A STAIN OF OUR PRESENCE

ON WHITSTABLE BEACH

I was the prince here: a small boy
in short trousers with a half-crown haircut,
striped school tie and his shirt-tail hanging out,
socks and shoes in hand for knee-deep paddling.
The beach has hardly changed: the Isle on the skyline,
the same oncoming waves, the same pebbles underfoot,
some flat and good for skimming, some stained
with tar, others glistening or masked in sand,
drilled clean through by tidal awls or sucked concave,
bird's-egg-speckled or veined like ore, red
and pink and green, slate-black or gullback-grey.
And this is the great stone, round and weighty,
which my father lifted with a swipe of his instep,
like a 50's centre scoring a goal from the circle,
to crash the shin of someone he'd thought leering at my mum,
the single time I saw my gentle dad disturb the peace.

Was it an ugly or a noble thing? I know the sun went in
and my parents didn't speak for the rest of the afternoon,
backs to the breakwater. With a million weapons all around,
the bones of my enemies half-buried in the mud,
                                        their destroyed craft still
thrashing in the waves and splintering,
                        I stood on the shore and stoned the sea.

DUNGENESS

The cross-tide discloses
a triangular acre of possibly radio-active mud,
not the right attributes for a beach.
The gulls are giant and ferocious,
having found something flayed
and succulent in the sea-garbage
which they dissect membrane by membrane.

The Jarman garden
sprouts rocky phallic circles;
the shingle-people rise like planted dragon's teeth,
slump-shouldered, lump-hipped Adams,
and cactus-Eves with spiny pads of breasts.
This isn't God's idea of a garden;
viper's bugloss wouldn't grow here if it were.

Donne's 'Busie old foole...'
is written on the tarred cottage wall, re-slanted
for a house of gay love. Contours change,
hard to decipher. They even had to build
three lighthouses as if they were uncertain of the shape,
though they got the power stations right first time -
Dungeness A and Dungeness B: squat and square and huge.

Away from all this,
two small boys, ten-year-old philosophers,
are lying daubed in mud on their stomachs,
discussing things with the sea breathing over them.
They are perfectly formed and perfectly innocent,
Archimedes and Aristotle in their youth.
We hope there's nothing nasty in the ooze.

THE TRIP TO THE WATERFALL

On the way to the waterfall, we passed the factory,
separated from the forest by concrete embankments,
jutting out on its vee of land into the river.
It was a mix of funnels, towers and buttresses,
storage tanks and sheds, linked by tubing. This gave way
to an area of shallow pools, frothing with suds,
raked by mechanical arms which drew back the foam
like a croupier's fork collecting the stakes.
We passed close enough
        to see the circular warnings posted on the fences,
bearing the images of snarling guard dogs. They moved
                              cinematically as
they flashed by us, on post after post of the long enclosure.

        Sitting together
        at the brow of the falls,
        we passed a bottle from hand to hand,
        the only ones
        to have made the climb.

        Later, we bathed,
        teetering on a threshold of rock,
        then lay re-christened
        like tribal look-outs
        above our land.

It was calm mid-afternoon when the plain below us
burst into flame at one point. It was quick and mute and remote.
If we had been nearer we would have heard the explosions
that ran from tank to tank, seen the trees laid flat
by the blast and the metal faces of the dogs buckle

and disintegrate. Instead, we stared without understanding,
removed by height from our own civilisation,
at the orange beacon and the smoke rising from it;
while, allowed to loll, our bottle tipped wine
continuous and dark, like a stain of our presence,
that travelled without our noticing
                              from
                                 top
                                    to
                                    bottom
                                       of
                                        the
                                          falls.

THE SPRINGS

Water surfaces from moss, from roots, from gravel,
from under the hill.
These days, the rains have turned the sprinklers on
and fed new rivers
all along the roads between the farms. The cars toss
dividing walls of spray
and for the first time in centuries, the cattle drink
at the old and holy springs.

Hermits wade thigh-deep in their caves, cupping
the spluttering drops
to their rough faces, muttering the rising of a prayer,
recalling how to heal.
The sick, blind and lame, and others none of these,
find submerged addresses,
descending in helicopters to the legendary fluids.
It is a cool and wet religion.

The distinctive tastes of secret passages to air,
clay, loam, lime, chalk,
are savoured by the connoisseurs; aquatic names,
Saint Thomas's well,
Brother Martin's flagon-fill, the Bare Sisters' pool,
claim authenticity.
Rare miracles occur. An archbishop stops by to bless.
A virgin gives birth in the waters.
One day, the rains cease. A darker patch of soggy land
remains, then dries in an August drought.

EMMENTAL

The hills, like buttresses of one another, rise
haunch by haunch, forcing the road to imitate their curves,
locking out the blocks and factories of the Basel plain.
I hitched a lift with a sour delivery man, who grumbled
at his route - "they ought to put a motorway through here" -
swerving through trim plots of forest, edged with hives,
past timber houses, their great roofs slanting to the ground,
a winter's wood stacked against the byres, his wheels verging
on slopes so steep they cannot be worked by modern machines.

Instead, we saw the implements of another century - scythes,
flails, horse-drawn ploughs - and whole families, heat-shackled,
labouring in the fields. He called them 'peasants',
added, 'slaves of the land' and laughed.
                              "Well," I said cautiously,
  "isn't it better to be that, than
          building, levelling, mining, spoiling
                    the masters of it?"

THE BEAR AND THE CITY

In a crook of the green Aare, the founding duke
set his city and named it from the first kill
his huntsmen made - a bear ambling down the hill
as if to greet them. Thus it became the mark
of ducal power, rampant on shields and flags.
Living emblems, cubs are kept in the street pits,
loved for their cuteness, begging for titbits
or chasing nose-to-tail through hollow logs.

Out of the past, spear-pierced, a rough, sham-
bling creature raises itself to human height
and roaring, as if a stake is driven tight
that pegs the city to the map, yields its name.

Dead once it has spoken, the bear is ours,
its space surrendered to fountains, arcades, towers.

MOTORWAY NEAR BASEL

Cars dominate, that leave rich Europe for the south,
D, F, NL, CH, washed showroom fresh
by earlier rain, with contoured flanks and slatted mouth
like bunched herds heading for the plateau-edge.
A farmhouse with geranium-crowded sills
is seen at speed as darkness streaked with blood;
it gathers shade, amid the buzz of racing devils,
its shutters closed, its eaves a swallowtail of wood.

Along the valley, the rising foothills of the Alps
are mined by tunnels, spanned by bridges, ringed about
by noise, though eased at times by random gaps
or temporary closure, as if a madness is cast out.
And once, looking from the house - 3 a.m., moonshine -
they saw, lying across the lanes, stilled, dreaming swine.

THE GREEN APE

Our camera whirred; her followers whooped,
some sullen at the back as if they had betrayed too much.
Thick with filth, hung with trinkets made of shell and bone,
the ape was carried shoulder-high on a makeshift litter
like an invalid noblewoman by her retinue.
Reclining there, she trapped a flea itching her thigh
or chattered in a mirror to the face she saw.
Through the forest, her bearers chanted in her praise;
later, after that last ceremony, they sold for a pittance
their sacred ape, cowering in her matted coat.

We scrubbed her clean, scraping off the clay
that clogged her fur, revealing as we rinsed
her rare colours - emerald, malachite, jade -
as if we panned them from a stream.
We touched uniqueness, delving to the roots,
watching, as the fear wore off, her face brighten,
a peering baby's wrapped in its green shawls.
She seemed to like the brush and comb, whimpering
when we touched by chance a tumour on her side,
a hidden fungus at the bottom of lush grass.

That tumour stank, polluting every camp we made
on the journey back. In the city hospital,
when drugs had failed to reduce its size,
the surgeon cut, splicing the flesh and making new.
The ape survived, to lead a different kind of life:
she sleeps in sheets, loves jewels and perfumes,
and sulks until she's bathed and groomed, using dyes
to stem the ebb of colour from her coat -
her pigment fading, her forest-habits gone,
the green ape lives,
                    but lives by our technique alone

THE LINEAGE OF APPLE TREES

The weather is benign in early October.
On the orchard floor are the apples
economics left to rot,
red striated with yellow,
bruised or gnawed hollow
or beak-pocked. One sound fruit
you can pick from the branch,
yielding to your palm,
an offering from the tree
as if it bribes you to be kind.

Your family that owned this land
go back more than two millennia;
they marched with the legions,
and, inter-marrying, settled here.
A medieval prioress, whose sisterhood
was drunk on cider;
a Georgian general who helped to lose America
but gave his name to this variety;
a Victorian canning magnate and his sister -
the lady explorer in skirts on a camel,

who, so they say, planted an espalier among the palms;
an admiral who fed his men on crates of eaters
until his ship split off the Azores.
Do Bedouin camp
beneath the blossom in the Sahara spring?
Did a fleet of migrant apples
bob to the tune of the Atlantic Ocean?
You bite through the peel and reach the core,
pocketing the pips before you turn.
The last of the line. Your hand signals the digger in.

IN THE TIME OF BIRD FLU

At dusk the bird-swarm hits the sky, for one
last crazy flight; hot-blooded skaters,
they carve their figures-of-eight again at dawn
after the silencing night's hiatus.

Issuing their calls of ownership and mating,
warbling a chanson to the air
or hidden in the bushes altercating...
We hardly note them, but they're there.

They give their name to this pandemic,
its shadow like a winged pestilence;
the birds don't know what makes them sick -
the fear is ours, not these rowdy innocents'.

We do our bit to aid the virus -
a hushed-up illness, a shady importer -
until it comes and raids the hen-house
or settles with the swan on sunlit water.

THE GREAT EXPLORER

Ten months a captive of the tribes,
he'd lowered his head and fed with cattle,
until one day they cut his tether. Their harsh
laughter told him nothing, why they'd held him
or why, now, they let him go. Was it pity
or mockery that the women bathed his sores,
tittering when they raised his white man's 'thing',
but later stoned him from the village, a ritual
exiling which purified their land of him?
Salt trails to the coast. A frigate. London.
That season's curiosity - his life with savages.

So, he made the second journey, fevered,
and, coming to the mangrove-choked river bend,
fell to a flutter of arrows from the shore.
In a trance, he tailed a roving band of ghosts,
dead warriors with clan-scars on their cheeks,
feeding on offerings left outside the huts.
They led towards the place he sought, the source
of journeys - water thundering from the rock,
fish teeming, where Africa gives birth to rivers
that flick their tails and vanish in a blaze of spray,
leaving him alone in scrub. Heat-flayed. Tribeless.

His statue stands in the town where he was born,
another where schooled - bronze mummy-cases,
cast by an imperial foundryman two centuries ago,
hollow, as if it might be true he walks the bush,
refusing to join the dead of his own people.
Others followed, dismantling kingdoms, cornering
markets, bartering for slaves along his routes.
But, told of townships and the lake named after him,
the honours awarded to his sons, the books written,
I know that his spirit does not reside in those wrappings,
nor is contained in bronze or marble,
            but flies with Swallowtail, flows with Nile.

TWO
NEARING A TEMPLE

THE FOX-RED GODDESSES

There the fox-red goddesses stand, a row of figurines
all belly, breasts and thighs, moulded out of clay
with narrow necks that wear ascending collars of gold
and hands that grasp on snakes. A gang of girls
in the charge of a prim mistress come to gaze:
some blush, some guffaw, others learnedly discourse
on cults of ancient Crete - and some give sly smiles
                              which show
they too have met, fox-red and naked in the dark
of cave-like rooms, serpents that come to be their slaves.

THE FIELD

A shoddy uncultivated field of clay
faced our house like an inland sea, plugging
the gap in a splay of streets. Its whole surface
was cut in ridges as if once ploughed; others said
somebody had been down on his knees by moonlight,
trying to hack out downward flights of stairs
to reach a goddess beneath the clods.
                    I passed it daily
on my way to school; it was dry and crumbling
in mid-summer or sucking at my heels in storms.
I found used condoms of local lovers there
and learnt its history, of Harry Old who shot himself
and Annie Jones, raped and strangled with her stocking.
Despite these casualties, I made the field my own,
mapping out roads along its furrows or hiding coins,
returning later to see if they had multiplied.

One spring the archaeologists came, who portioned it off
with posts and string, sinking a city at different levels
of shallow cellars that rain flooded. They found some tiles
and shards, the same red ochre as the land, a Roman lintel,
a Saxon pin, a Tudor buckle, a Georgian spoon...
                    I was sorry
when they left, the surface smoothed, the diggings closed,
sure that I could have ducked beneath their boundaries
and raised the goddess from her floor of clay.

ANUBIS

*According to medieval legend, St Christopher wished to be
a dog in order to resist the wiles of the seductresses. This
Christian story is influenced by remnants of Egyptian myth
concerning Anubis, usually represented by a dog's head.*

I am the dog, Anubis,
a skull-white head.
I have been pared by the desert
to an empty socket of bone
and when I put on flesh once more,
I shall not know my mistress.

Laila and Jezebel, the seductresses,
with red fingernails and kohl-rim eyes,
sidled up to Christopher and asked him,
"will you come to dance and drink with us?"
So Christopher put on his dog's-head coat
and sailed out into the night with them,
one on each arm, and let them tempt him
with all the pleasures of their Babylon.

 I am the dog, Anubis,
a barking head.
I am black and powerful.
If these vixens touch me,
I shall snap off their tails
with my sharp Egyptian teeth.

Back in their flat, he allowed them both
to loosen his coat and slide their palms
across the silky fur of his perfumed armpits,
his aching groin, the little cross of black
on his flat belly. His cock rose to them
but he would not pay to enter their bodies,
preferring to think how brave he lay there,
resisting the temptresses, Jezebel and Laila.

I am the dog, Anubis,
a yapping head.
If you tickle my belly,
I shall roll over
and grin with all my teeth
but I shall not follow you.

Laila and Jezebel grew tired of playing
with the stubborn proud man, Christopher,
who would not slough off his dog's-head coat.
Laughing, they showered together, embracing
like sisters in the fiercely jetting water
that washed their bodies lithe and clean
of the paints and lotions and Assyrian oils.
There, through half-closed eyes, he watched.

I am the dog, Anubis,
a snoozing head.
I shall lie down and sleep
like a blind old hound
but I shall wake terrible
 in the sun of my master.

Jezebel and Laila turned around and saw,
rising above them, Christopher with a knife,
sweat-gleams on his brow, ready to sacrifice
to some god that demanded it in his head.
They kneeled and bowed and, as they did so,
he glimpsed the tender flesh of their napes,
like all the children he might have fathered,
and taking off his coat, he wrapped them safe.

I am the dog, Anubis,
a faithful head.
I am of ancient pedigree.
I shall kill the she-lynx
but the children of my master
I shall love and protect them well.

When the strange thick-pelted man had gone,
the two women shivered in each other's arms;
they painted again in their bright mirrors
and went into the streets of unknown people,
their nerve-ends tingling, blood trembling,
in case they might see his face in the crowd.
But Christopher had gone on other journeys
and would only remember them when he died.

I am the dog, Anubis,
a swimming head,
nearing a temple on the bank;
when I reach it, I shall shake
the Nile out of my red coat
and find our Isis in her shrine.

FISH

after a painting by Sara Wicks

Fish went walking
up the slope of the shingle to the land,
his gills craving, his tail stiff with leverage,
heaving his body against the scaly trunks of the palms,
his brothers on the shore with whom he danced.
This is today's miracle,
          a fish walking on land.

Tomorrow I shall tell you another tale: the woman
who lives underneath the sea, walking upside down
on fingertips on the parti-coloured sand,
her lungs beating like a heart, her heart gulping,
a stream of bubbles rising from her lips to where the air is.

The woman hides inside a clam; fish sings,
under the shadow of the fronds; tree-frogs
watch the hang-gliding bats and think,
'One day we'll do that too, but until then...'

Lovers exchange oxygen, babies float
in amniotic calm while they may,
          while rocks sway,
                    while sun
lights the lagoon night and moon the sand-dune day.

THE CAVES AT AJANTA

- decorated by Buddhist monks, 200 BC - 200 AD

More like the name of a religion than a state,
Maharashtra gives tiny miracles among infinities,
a wedding procession banging and tooting in a village,
the poorest women possessing the beauty of the saree.
From Mumbai to Ajanta, I saw the clockwise swastik,
the mark of Surya, daubed for luck on doors and lorries,
Sanskrit not Nazi, my lexicon of signs reversed.
The sun is Maharashtra's god, blessing at morning,
pardoning at evening, not swallowed in the great eclipse
but beating with the energy that drives the road.

In one of the painted vaults of Ajanta,
the guide said: "Here, the echo's good."
The walls swelled the volume of his chant
that boomed the names of God or gods.
I thought of Forster. In these airy temples,
he might reverse the message of the Marabar,
blessed by the image of the Bodhisattva,
peeling but golden, seen by reflected light
as if it graced the dark of Plato's cave.
The India he loved is here, the echo good.

Mumbai, alias Bombay, added me to its millions,
both names as rounded as the breasts and haunches
of the dancing girls and courtesans the monks depicted
when they turned their painter-eyes towards the world.
Their fragile but surviving art would compass this:
the stump-armed beggars, prostitutes in slum-cages,
the glittering bay, the towers of wealth at Nariman,
the street faces. Each one's a question since Ajanta.
"Are you he?" "Are you she?"
                    Throughout the world,
            the Bodhisattva follows me with his eyes.

THE LAMB OF GHENT

- The Ghent Altarpiece

Jan van Eyk called it
the Mystic Lamb - I call it
The Miracle of the Human Face.

No demon's grimace or smug
Madonna's vapid smile - only
the ripening look of grace

in Adam, Eve, Maria, John,
in the Son and the Father
gazing out of the one countenance.

And in the centre, the lamb itself,
a stocky Flemish sheep,
radiating gold in the weavers' city.

The guidebook calls it
an image of redemption - I call it
something more local and important.

It is there in the forty-two
botanically perfect flowering plants,
the stepped gable seen through a window,

the crystal stem of God's sceptre
as it catches the world's light -
if you ask the question "What is Art?"
this is the answer of Jan van Eyk.

SI CHIN'S CELLULAR AUTOMATA

The poem describes a work of art by Si Chin Liu, a perspex
box which gives the illusion of infinite perspectives

Plate of perspex layered onto perspex plate,
sliced as thin and accurately as lenses,
and, in the centre, a sheaf of perspex rods.
Their chamfered tips construct a pyramid,
its razor angles astronomically determined
according to the hourly progress of the sun
across a year's arc of world. This is called
      Si Chin's cellular automata,
a twelve-month to calculate, a month to make.
A low square box packed with time and space.

Switch off the lights. Play a torch-beam.
Angles alter. Pyramid liquefies and shifts.
If there is an old-time bearded God who had
a lone front seat at the autonomous creation,
he must have witnessed something like this,
not the heaving of mountains, valleys, plains,
but through a divine electron microscope
      the cellular blueprints.
It seems sterile - it breeds everything.
A small square box, the magic universal womb.

The architect of this microcosm is watching,
her passive face mooned by reflected light
as the torch strikes upwards from the mystery
to meet the mystery of flesh, waxing, waning,
cheeks as plump as day, eyes as sharp as night.
But it's her device that concentrates our gazes -
the structured rods are stretching lawlessly
      in a box a quarter-metre square
down down down down down down down
further than China or the infinite frontiers.

THREE
AND THEN NOT SEEN AGAIN

CIRCLES

Circles repeat themselves, the diminishing
eddies of the vortex, swiftly narrowing
to a centre where it pulls the vessel down.
When the captain is first caught, he panics
and tries to swim out, but the whirlpool
has him like an insistent limpet lover,
whose face he is not yet sure of, then
he enters calm water and thinks of escape
but the next eddy claims him and takes him
again in the same path; he panics less,
is less ecstatic when the depths clamp him,
learns to recognise the sanity of the pause
before the third and then the fourth...

It needs many orbits before he loses consciousness/
It needs many orbits before he gains consciousness/

and submits to what has been trying to claim him/
and realises what it is that has been trying to claim him/

all the time, Charybdis who had seen and loved him far off/
all the time, twirling Charybdis disappearing into herself/

and plotted her maritime traps for him under the cliff/
while lurking Scylla dwindles to a smudge on the horizon/

Scylla who will devour the drifting wreckage and crew. /
and he is left floating on an open sea after the storm.

THE CHECK DIGIT

My information keeps on adding up to you
but, when I check, the answer's always wrong.
Some of the data must have been corrupt,
a chain so long I can't unscramble it
to find the misread digit,
            the item out of true.

The code I thought I'd understood
refuses to unlock the vault. Instead,
it trips alarms. Totals disintegrate
as spy-cameras scan for decoys,
for love's impersonators
            who infiltrated.

That final number, impassive, stubborn,
floors each re-count. The error's mine,
unless, somewhere along the line,
the figures cheated on us, switching
identities, and sabotaged
            the perfect sum.

* The check digit is the number at the end of a series, a total
against which the accuracy of the calculation can be checked.
If the check digit fails to match, an error must have been
introduced.

THE HAIR

I hardly knew you when, mid-afternoon,
standing behind you in the office doorway,
I picked a hair from your shoulder
    and you turned
with such a lazy familiar smile
you seemed to acknowledge all our past lives together.

That was years ago, near Christmas,
a memory of my fingertips, your nape,
and we have scarcely met since then;
    but there has been
that thread between us, the one time
we touched counting more than any lover in our beds.

A CHINESE WORD

It is called in Chinese
love-between-passers-by.

They cross in the street,
going to their own destinations.

Chance synchronises them.
If one is late, the other is too.

They acknowledge each other with a discreet grace
like adulterers who are introduced as strangers.

The word also conveys the fact
(without a hint of whether this is happy or sad)

that they never pursue the friendship.
Perhaps it is inconvenient. Or unnecessary.

They learn one of the tricks of life,
to know the difference between accident and fate.

AT CHESIL

Ten-metre breakers are charging Chesil Bank,
chaos theory in action, this land, this lagoon,
created by criss-cross forces of no intent
except to jostle, a territory of disturbances,
a formlessness capable of such fine distinctions
that each pebble is graded by its position on the shore.

Between the 1300s and now, a monster's four times
surfaced off the beach, half fish, half sea-horse,
not hard to explain - cheap lure for tourists,
a drunken man's hallucination, a hoax, an error.
Or did a conjunction of the tides and winds,
a random pattern of the waves, a special frequency,

produce an excitement in the brain to match?
We saw the monster, which, being seen, existed,
as tall as a tall ship, as vast as a stone hill,
had attributes - a crest, fangs, scales, claws, fins.
It was there, as undeniable as love on the four occasions
it was seen and then not seen again.

                              Just vacancy. Just sea.

ENTRAILS

Everything happened as in stories it should -
love, marriage, babies, the spark always igniting
    first time, life going somewhere good,
pulling us as if we trailed on a lucky kite-string,
keeping us clear of danger or even the need to think.
    Who would have questioned what we'd got?
Perhaps that is how we failed to register the stink,
the yelp, of the vixen in the entrails of the plot.

We found her on the heath. A hot day in the ferns.

Proudly, we thought we had tamed something wild;
others bickered and divorced or else hardened
    into indifference while we smiled,
the cub licking our hands in the walled garden.
Things imploded. Let's skip the sordid details,
    neurosis and counter-neurosis, psychic
splinters that stabbed us, here, in the entrails
where the captive vixen gnawed, her last sly trick.

Her claws scrape on flesh as, cornered, she turns.

We need a surgeon to sew us, one clever enough
to disguise the scars, so our friends never see
    the pain in our bellies; we'll bluff
our way through to a kind of mutual equanimity;
unless, displaying our wounds to the world after all -
    not caging or splaying or slaying her,
or mounting her rigid grin to taunt us on our wall -
we let her run free from our lives, not staying her,
and wait to discover for what purpose she returns
    if, in the night-hours, she wakes and burns.

THE CAT AND THE MOTH

I was new to the office and he was my boss,
a greying man with cat-slanting eyes;
after two days he asked me, without any fuss,
if I'd come to his flat and dine with him there.
I suppose that I'm different from those other girls
who keep clear; I'd decided since school
to live for my pleasure as my rule in the world
and so - for my pleasure - I answered his call.
And after the meal, with his wine in my head,
I went on his arm up the stairs to his bed.

He warned me and then he began to undress
until I could see a thorny raised scar
up thigh, groin and rib. This twist in his flesh
was something - he shrugged - that he got in the war.
We had sex. It was good as he'd said,
but while he was sleeping, I kept on the lamp
to stare at the scar and imagine it red
in the thick of the battle or the prisoners' camp.
I was ready to flinch when I drew my hand down
as if, like a rash, the scar was passed on.

Next day when I saw him all dressed up in clothes,
as sleek as a cat that has licked down its pelt,
I found with relief I forgot when I chose
the hard ridge of pain I had felt
and, changing my job, I never went back.
But when I've got naked for some other man,
while he's arching my body and nibbling my neck,
I've looked sideways and seen, familiar to me,
in my moth-like reflection in mirrors or panes,
the trace of a scar, like a pattern on wings.

HERO'S COUSIN

- an alternative plot-line to <u>Much Ado</u>

'I'm here,' she says. I look up from my thoughts
and see her at the door. Hero — pretty Hero! —
confidently returned for her rightful husband.
I remember her sitting in the green tent of a willow
and discussing young Claudio gone off to the wars
with Benedict his friend; babbling of the wedding;

then suddenly dead in a faint and the family telling me
I had to get dressed for the church because...
Am I going to be his? Is he going to be mine?
...because there had to be a substitute. They made me
wear her scents, heels that brought me to her height,
tighter lacing for Hero's narrowness at the waist.

I hid behind the veil and waited. He lifted it.
The light fell on my face. I didn't miss a blink.
I wanted to see the disappointment and I did,
his pupils dilating as he took it in - a wider gap
between the teeth, nose slightly hooked, an eye askew,
millimetre discrepancies that made the difference

between beauty and beauty's cousin, ugliness.
He half-turned to blame the father, then recalled
what he owed. "A second Hero!" he exclaimed.
At first he took me for his punishment, blurting
her name into the pillow as he flooded me.
Later he took me for his joy. I'd skills she never had.

'I didn't die,' she explains, 'I've been in the convent,
learning how to forgive.' My Claudio looks blankly.
The gap between the teeth is perfect, her lips cherry.
'Wife, give your cousin dinner while I'm out —
I'm seeing Benedict at *The Cock*. Escaping B!'
I don't mind the consolatory jokes (I'm the Gargoyle,

Bea's the Shrew), a drunken return at three a.m.,
a snuggling kind of sex and gossip in bed about that pair.
I'm turning to offer a drink but she has faded from the house
as if she might have been my dream. Back to the nuns?
This is an ending different from all those endings
we imagined when we were girls and they were boys.

* In 'Much Ado About Nothing', Claudio, after he has been tricked into falsely
accusing his bride-to-be, Hero, of unfaithfulness and has caused her apparent
death, agrees to marry Hero's cousin. In fact, his new bride, the 'cousin', is
Hero herself, who has only pretended to be dead. This poem imagines that he is
obliged to marry her actual cousin as recompense for his false accusation.

FOUR

THE LOWER REGIONS

THE HONEY-BUCKET MAN

I

The seventh day, the brochure said, was 'Tour Up-Country'. At the cross roads
where our village started, traffic zoomed, as if it mowed the forest back,
while on the verge, parked unaccountably, were lorries with tarpaulined loads.
There - while we watched though motioned by our guide towards the track -
the drivers bargained at a roadside stall. Drawn like disobedient kids
to discover the enticement, we went closer and viewed the trestles
littered with trash: cigarette cases with now-dead filmstars on the lids,
ballpoint pens already leaking, scissors loose at the shanks, plastic whistles.
Looking up, we saw, beneath an awning of green and yellow stripes, the stall's
real treasure, wad on wad, clipped on hoarding, calendars in cellophane wraps
bearing photos of long-thighed, callipygous, bare-breasted girls
whose Western flesh seduced the small-framed camioneurs.

We took our snaps,
angling for the jungle backdrop, the tin-roofed huts and tall grasses
that made the shot unique. The trader grinned, his hair slicked
in a Presley wave, a tout in open-necked white shirt and dark glasses,
who asked for payment - "dollar, please" - each time a shutter clicked.

Within the village, we wandered freely, treating it as our own,
like a film-set we had hired. Our cameras aimed at everything, upwards
at a boy squatting on a balcony, into shadows at a crone,
through gaps in fences at the hogs and fowl and children in the yards.
Behind some shacks, against the forest, a man stood by an open pit.
"Who's that?" I asked the guide, who paused, then bashfully translated,
"Honey-bucket man". In other words, bent, half-blind, he ladled shit,
transferring it to metal containers in a cart. The task completed,
he placed himself between the shafts, his clothes spattered, his legs slimed,
as if, born to that job, he'd paddled in feculence since a child.

Back in the capital, a revolution threatened with gunfire our ill-timed
holiday. Our coach was stoned by youths who yesterday we'd photo-ed mild,
now fierce as demons in a play.

        That night, the President made an urgent broadcast,
but chose, pursuing an advantage that he saw, to feed the blaze
with further slogans. "The foreigners destroy our nation, plunder our past,
defile our women, corrupt our youth, exploit our people as their slaves."
All Western visitors would be expelled, all Western goods were banned,
he stated; and then, his voice rising at the end of the harangue, he bayed:
"no more Western filth!" - a chant in which his audience joined until,
as if their clamour overloaded the airwaves, our radio went dead.

Scrawny under rags, the honey-bucket man came murmuring,
                        'buy, buy, my black gold,'
and led me through his dark to teeter on the mud-edge of the pit;
there I saw, torn images on stained paper, the faces of the girls the stall had sold,
their breasts and thighs like parts of corpses, bullet-riddled or throats slit.

The room-phone woke me - a flight had been arranged, leaving towards dawn.
Below us, as we rose beyond the blocks and temples, the terraced fields of rice,
the trader occupied a local prison cell, his calendars condemned to burn,
or, shrewder, had left the roadside for a snug upholstered office
where, haggling over prices, phoning to the States,
                       bribing customs men and judges,
he planned black market operations that would multiply his wealth;
and in the villages, unremarked, where dozens gathered round a single radio
                   to listen to the speeches,
the honey-bucket man joined in the zealous chanting:
                   "No more filth! No more filth!"

DRAGONS

He killed that night for the tenth time,
having followed her through fog for miles.
Drinking later in a small bar,
he watched the faces of the murdered girls
stare lifeless out of a TV blur
while someone read the catalogue of names -
a hard shell that he wore like scales,
in which he breathed like fire.

Through doors that opened at her tread,
she entered the displays of jewels,
her fingers flickering in air.
Her bright reflections also stole,
that moved with her through the store
and multiplied her risk in glass -
a hard shell that she wore like scales,
in which she breathed like fire.

The children formed a clenched group,
with cigarettes held like short spears
against the questions of the law.
The body lay beneath the stairhead rails.
Nobody pushed him, Sir, they swore,
each one harboured by the others' lies -
a hard shell that they wore like scales,
in which they breathed like fire.

MR LARIMER'S LESSON

There were times I doubted I was sane; I had seen you
at the top of those dowdy stairs and reeled at just
the beauty of your profile, something proud and defiant
in the jut of your lip, the angle of your brow sloping
into the broad flared nose, a physiognomy so generous
I should have known you'd write with kisses on the seal,
to 'Mr Larimer, Room 7, the School', telling me all --
college, job, the flat, the shy formal men who looked
at you as I had done as if you were a carnal dream.
It'd gone no further. I was thirty-four and you were seventeen,
teacher and pupil. You teased, I ached. I reached, you shied.
And bullied three terms long, friendless Billy Bressup cried.

I did not answer - my wife would not have understood -
and resolutely left the next unread. But you wrote on
with the chatty innocence of notes passed secretly in Maths:
how you were gaining weight, about to get engaged,
had had a modelling portfolio done but no luck yet…
Added to lust, the greater guilt of love arrived,
a trifold sin as if, by neither replying nor telling,
I betrayed my wife, myself and you. Each blithe scrawl,
sometimes none for years, then a spate, then none again,
convicted me of a ten-year adultery I'd failed to commit.
At last I wrote a secret letter back. My heart drooled.
And Billy Bressup, grown, was pinned in nightmare to the school.

Well, here I am, with thinning hair and scrawny neck,
wishing I could halve my age to yours, and there you,
to my surprise, the bouncy kid dressed up in glamour,
teeth flashing, eyes on fire with a torch of wonderings,
confiding tales of your last three fiancés, idiot
young men, that make us roar as if at Chaucer fabliaux.
My careful role, proud uncle treating his favourite niece,
slips to drunken lecher, sliding my hand along your thigh.
Restaurant and classroom spin. 'O Mr Larimer.' you croon,
'I've wanted you so long.' I pay the bill and off we go,

teacher and pupil, schooled to forget for one wild night
that Billy Bressup,

    who I might have loved instead of you,
                had dowsed his clothes and set himself alight.

MOTHER AND CHILD

We were driving at thirty down Cambridge Hill
when, on a bike, her kid against the handle-bars,
this girl, not more than eighteen, grubby, small,
freewheeled through and shot the junction. The cars
went loco, swerving, hooting, brakes slammed hard,
but she just nervelessly looked back, one finger
in the air. The child whooped. She never veered,
arrow-straight for the next crossroads and its danger.

If they die, they'll die cheaply. A broom and bucket
will clear the tarmac of the feckless bitch and brat.
Better that, than leave us always on the look-out,
never knowing when they will pop up on the left or right
and send us into the path of a juggernaut head-on -
while they survive, riding on gravity through Armageddon.

THE PRAGUE CLOCK

- the designer of the intricate clock in Prague was
blinded by order of the council so that he could
not work for rival cities; in revenge, he destroyed
the mechanism.

The blinded maker staggers with the blow of the hammer
that smashes his finest art;
strikes again so that his clock
shall not strike the hours
of the petty men who ordered it and thought it theirs.
Now he is proving it his,
at the cost that, when they find him, amidst the wreckage
like a wound-down automaton,
blood is weeping from his sockets and his heart is ticking
so slowly that it counts
the centuries until the Spring
snaps under the revenge of tanks and time again goes missing.

If the Hamelin burghers' fit of peevish ingratitude
lost them their offspring,
all except the lame and sick,
did this jealous blunder lead
to Kafka measuring his dick, the Fascist burning of the Square,
the prisoners rotting in Bartolomy,
to the melancholia that flowed as drunkenly as the Vltava
in Soldier Schweyk and Fireman's Ball?
Was nothing possible until the tourists with their magic purses,
snapping the hourly puppet-show,
chattering like returned children,
brought back Time to what at last has been restored? -

Prague.

from IN SICILIA

THE MADONNA OF SCIACCA

- for Christine, Francesco, Alessandro and Enrico

One hundred barefoot fishermen,
grimacing, sweating, fighting for position,
their upbent arms like the oars of a galley,
row the Madonna over the heads of the crowd.
If she totters as she comes from the cathedral,
the harvest and the catches will be poor.
This year, she glides.

> *Madonna, O Madonna,*
> *gilded and groomed for your one outing of the year,*
> *accompanied by music and rowdy devotion,*
> *gifted with money by those you have healed,*
> *look on a stranger -*
> *what I am asking is a miracle of the heart.*

Bearing her in her howdah through the streets,
with night falling and her image lit in gold,
they salute the sea and then the quarters of the town.
Children hold fairground balloons - winged horse, dolphin,
swordfish.
Rock begins in the square and bonfires on the beaches.
American returnees run the festival again on camcorders.
Old women sleep happy, their lives illumined
from the time they were daughters
to the time that they rule their sons' marriages.
The power of the Madonna is locked away for another year.

PHILIP OF THE HEADS

The returned immigrant,
addled by the USA,
shut himself in a rocky place
and carved
tiered ramparts of faces in a savage style
with gash and gouge for mouths and eyes,
a jumbled history
of crowned dukes and crazed mosaicists,
cannibals and prodigals,
inquisitors and informers,
all reduced to grins or scowls.

The Yanks had called him "wop" and "headcase".
The locals called him "Philip of the Heads".
The heads called him "Your Excellency".

PIAZZA MARINA, PALERMO

A madman is pacing among the ancient banyan trees,
raising his voice as if he calls across the sea
to the sharks gathering to breed in a secret place,
to the lookout monkeys in the high palms
        on the Carthaginian coast: "Papa! Papa!"
They hear him in Tripoli and Rabat.
        They do not hear him in Lombardy and Rome.

THE HOUSE OF PIRANDELLO

- Agrigento

1.
Up on the walls
of the Casa Natale of Pirandello,
there are blow-ups of the playwright
with his friends of Rome (but not Benito),
framed playbills - Paris, London, New York -
like the destinations of shipping lines
for immigrants from Sicily;
there is the Stockholm letter
(buffoonery, he said)
and a trick photograph
in which Pirandello strokes his beard
watching Pirandello at the Remington,
one of them the Agrigentan,
one of them the international star.
2.
At the bottom of the garden
of the Casa Natale of Pirandello,
a long path's length from the house,
the pine where he loved to write,
where his ashes are interred,
has been blasted by winds,
a dead crown of naked branches
(Netta was his mad wife
and this was his tree).
I lean on the trunk,
thinking of Mr Rochester,
of what might be the linking power,
until Papa Luigi throws an inkstand at my head
and says: "Englishman, do not be absurd."

3.

The small estate
of the Casa Natale of Pirandello
belonged to the sulphur magnate,
his father; when the mines flooded,
his patrimony was lost,
his wife went crazy,
and he was cast into the twentieth century
like Lucifer plunging up to Hell -
Rome, Mussolini, a dud Nobel -
but kept the tatters of his wings
and flew from time to time
to the volcanic island of Sicily,
the lower region where his plays were born,
where writers leave the womb with tail and horns.

ERICE

- a mountain city where the fertility goddess was worshipped

With the mist blowing in at a thousand metres,
consuming the city, the white doves
are the only sign of the concealed goddess.
Aphrodite, Venus, Dea Eterna -
remembered in the names of pastry-shops and cafes
for tourists pregnant with money-belts -
has gone from the streets of churches and monasteries
and hidden her nakedness in a cloud.

But all night in my hotel room,
down in the heat of the Shell of Gold,
a dozen channels showed stripping call-girls -
"hot Sicilian ragazza, ring me, ring me..." -
holding the receiver to nipple and groin.
The sacred prostitutes of Astarte.

THE VALLEY OF THE TEMPLES

At the temple of Hera, I expected to find you,
where women complain of their faithless husbands,
but the heat was too great. From where you lay,
in a villa garden under a fig tree or a willow,
I must have been one of the dots on a hillside
as you watched the tourists among the columns,
crushed in the thumb and forefinger of the sun.
Perhaps you pitied them, not knowing that you pitied me.

SELINUNTE

The ruins
make romantic places,
a bleached temple standing on the headland,
fallen columns where we clamber like nursery children.
Someone tells a story
of how the Carthaginians shipped elephants from Africa
and took these cities. No-one has certainly identified
the temples. They are known as 'A' to 'O'.

That night, when we are eating ice-cream at the spa,
with a duo singing Sinatra songs to keyboard and sax,
a column of tanks rumbles by along the seafront,
so close we can touch the cladding. Manouevres.
It takes a quarter of an hour to pass.
Someone tells a story of how America bombed Afghanistan
and started World War Three. The ruins
make romantic places. Here, they ate ice-cream.

A ROMAN BATH

I was up to my shoulders in the warm waters,
a hot spring from Sicily's sulphurous underground,
when the men appeared, sharp suits, dark glasses,
the snouts of guns poking from their stubby fists,
yesterday's caricatures turned real and present.

We'd made the wrong friend – Domenico - who'd
brought us here to show the ruins in the hills:
an altar, columns, ancient roads the goats use,
and then *'il bagno Romano'*, a chance to stand in history
as tender and enveloping as fluids of the womb.

We'd rather liked our amiable guide, though not enough
to stay and argue out his case. Was it a land feud
or being found in the wrong bed or just a killing?
We fled, pounding across a flinty field of stones
to where we'd left our own van parked. It wasn't us

they wanted as they fired from habit or for fun,
sending the bullets scudding round our heads,
before they trussed him and shoved him in their car,
as dead already as if they'd shot him through the heart.
We drove fast towards the port, realising only on the ferry,
out of Messina,
      that our feet bled,
         that our shoes were full of warm blood.

CITY OF THE MONKS

Far back, the monks praying at its foundation, based
in a crook of the river where the fens forgot the mountains,
heard God bid them live among disease and annual disaster.
Chanting along the causeways, kneeling on rock in vigils,
they expelled the demons, who had lived in the miasma
and had loved to take the form of naked women, slimed
with river weeds, crumbling to corpse-dust in the bed.
But still their ewes, weakened by flukes from stagnant
waters, dropped stillborn lambs across the grey pasture.
They lost psalteries to mould and wooden saints to rot.
When cellars flooded, they baled them out. Survived on eels
and baked roots. Died before they had much time for sin.

The ducal engineers
drained the marsh
and built palaces,
fortresses and vaults.
They drove the monks elsewhere,
to moors and crags,
but in their memory
named the city after them.

The holy settlement has grown to secular magnificence –
banquets of goods, carpets of turf and flowering draperies
in the avenues and parks, tourist-flocks at the famous tower
and the icon-museum, wittier graffiti than in a capital.
Still, there are echoes if you walk particular squares at night,
a crazed voice bouncing off stone; a corpse-green tart
naked except for hat and jewels in the foyer of one of the great
                              hotels,
until you blink and remove the image; a shuttered train
with shadowed eyes between the slats; a synagogue in flames.
It was sometimes hard, by flares on the marshes, to distinguish
cowled monk from hooded devil. One survived all exorcism.
His claw-mark is in the history books. He clutched this city.

A MAN SWAM THE BLUE-GREEN KALE

That country, deciding to be an island, though no-one there
had ever seen a flounder or a sprat, made an effort of national cartography,
drawing and re-drawing its coastline in shapes according to the popular vote,
one month a famous actress's pudenda,
                            another month a bird-like spread of wings.

Coastguard stations and lighthouses were built along these contours,
with causeways carried out on stilts above the waves of black loam.
                                            Singing nautically,
trawlermen cast nets from tractors. A range of hills impersonated whales.
Transcontinental lorry-drivers had to obey the laws of international navigation,
steering among the buoys on the motorways, passing signs that warned:
'Danger submerged rocks'. Across the fields of marine cabbages,
travellers on rafts poled against the tides. A man swam the blue-green kale.

The country's neighbours, holding an emergency convention on the mainland,
declared all this 'an act of geographical lunacy'. In the cause of reason,
their tanks set out, and, more successfully than Pharaoh's troops
attempting the Red Sea, made the crossing with little difficulty,
although frogmen's suits and landing craft had been brought along
                                            as a precaution.
When the president was dragged out of his flagship, either to be shot
or put on trial in his admiral's uniform, (I forget which -
history changed so quickly in those days,
        the disappearance of islands was a common phenomenon)
he shouted: 'CHEATS! YOU ARE ALL DROWNED!' And nobody laughed.
In fact for years since then, the people of that country sniffed the air for salt
until the ocean rose, murdering the horizon, to come back
                                            crashing on their shores.

BRITANNIA'S DAUGHTER

- 2003

Brit was my name. I spent a stretch
inside Big Brother's house, I took my tits out
for Page Three, I won a million in a quiz.
I went out clubbing on vodka, sex and E's,
and smashed my new red racer up - then lights out.
A year on life support after they cut me from the wreck.

And all that while, the world was changing,
unknown to me. Men were plotting in distant
places. Votes got mysteriously discounted.
Towers fell. Hawks had the excuse they wanted.
War was the new reality show. Nothing pleasant
or green showed through the desert blizzards raging

Discharged, I reach into the past to find a home -
the hilltop path that gives a first view of the sea,
the grey upland farm on an edge of chalky fields.
My ancient, hardy mother waits; puts by her shield,
her spear, her armour, but finds no words to succour me.
Inside, hearts beat together; outside, a thickening gloom.

WAR

At one of her nipples there is a snake,
at the other a cockerel; at one
the dry gums, the other a horn beak.

She found them fighting and tried
to bring peace, giving them both
her milk in the garden in the cool shade.

But tugging long after they are slaked,
her sons suck her teats raw, one
with his dry gums, the other his horn beak.

SHADES OF WAR

- autumn 2004

I walk in the gardens,
on the run from the news.
The orange waste-sacks,
bellied with swept leaves,
crouch between the limes
all along the bare avenue -
prisoners of Guantanamo.

I walk in the orchards,
abandoned to autumn.
A dog leaps playful
out of its owner's control,
runs with the leash trailing
among the shit-coils in the dirt -
barking an echo of Abu Ghraib.

I walk in the break-time,
see poems on a classroom wall,
Owen, Sassoon, Sorley,
the texts of this year's syllabus:
words wailing like shells,
beyond the limits of our hearing -
mourning the corpses of Fallujah.

FIVE

THE APPROACH OF DARKNESS

THE ARCH AND ITS SHADOW

suggested by a painting by Mike Iddon

When I passed through the arch,
I did not see the shadow,
I was looking so hard into the light.

Someone was hidden in the side-darkness,
plucking my sleeve and asking for pity
where the stone stank of drunkards' piss.

The entered city was in celebration,
with ten-storey flags on the buildings
and marching bands in quartered uniforms.

A woman waited in a clearing in the crowds,
and said, as if she made a proclamation:
"Darling, this is our Independence Day."

I was speaking that night to the wedding guests,
full of the confidence of successful passage,
thinking again of the arch-top statuary,

the winged horses of joy and hope -
when suddenly half of my vision was darkened
and I could not remember my bride's name.

Then I ran to the city rim and slept out
on the paved threshold of the hills
where the arch and its shadow were one.

MARY AMONG THE DIAGRAMS

A school run by nuns. 'Girls, turn to page sixteen
and look at Figure One…' Not frog-on-a-log
from toytown lily-ponds, but Mister Toad with his jacket
rolled back, ready for surgery, the organs labelled
like parts of a computerised doll, to be disjoined.
'There's always one who faints,' said Sister Ann,
as Mary dropped the blade, aware as in a vision
of a phantom incubus, lodged below her heart,
with doubled haunches and smears of gold for eyes,
born out of thrust and jelly, quarrelling with the teacher's voice:
    Frog in the dish, foetus in the womb,
    I am
the flesh that hates the knife, the incarnation of the diagram.

Home for vacation, she found her grandmother tugging down
the ranked rose-trees, dismantling the quincunx
with all the passion of senility. Trellis by trellis,
the summerhouse of blossoms fell. Since her youth,
she'd tended and renewed the garden; now she screamed,
'Fuck the roses!' as Mary tried to lead her in,
palms bleeding, her eyes candescent, as if her memory
was burning with a golden flame that lit her skull.
A pyre of blueprints. Years later, it would flare in Mary,
dry-eyed at her child's funeral, and sear across the preacher's
voice:
    Canker in the bud, virus in the brain,
    I am
the crone in the rose-garden, the erasure of the diagram.

THE AMSTERDAM WIDOWER

The widower had come to Amsterdam not because
he wanted to escape his grief or thought
the years together cancer had robbed them of
might be reclaimed as the Dutch had reclaimed land;
rather that something in the flat brisk city
might match his mood, teach him to live
without a soul as the prostitutes did behind glass.

He had not expected so much light and space
rising from the water, the distorted shapes
of another city of rippling brightness,
gables, towers, his own figure on the bridge,
the hulls of barges, all as shining as her face
had shone through the dozen years - friendship,
courtship, a marriage without children, even dying.

Alone in Amsterdam, he'd thought he'd try
an equal dozen ways of murdering those years -
porno films, drugs, allowing himself to be enticed
by the displayed girls, beautiful and grotesque,
rattling at their casements like caged animals
to attract attention, winking, 'Come, I'll make
the scarlet tulip bloom from your withered corm.'

Instead, he lay in the still-new emptiness
of the hotel bed, wanting just the one woman
out of life's millions, just as she had wanted him.
Her diary told him that; yes, there had been lovers,
both friends of his, but he had understood.
It was in her nature to follow need and in
her nature to come back to him. She always did.

Around nine, he went downtown. An empty restaurant,
a Javanese waiter who soon stopped chatting.
He looked up and saw her in the opposite chair.
She smiled familiarly. A presence so real
he dropped his gaze and ate with the old relish.
This was just one more meal that they shared,
her face lit by his, his by her, wordless love.

He smoked after coffee, watching without regret
the apparition fade. A small cat that must
have been sleeping curled there all the time
raised its head above the table level and crossed
the cloth to lick his fingers, pink-tongued,
curvetting flirtily.
          The Javanese hurried to remove it.
'Don't,' he said, 'it's been my unseen company.'

That night, he was with his wife. The dream
created itself until he woke,
his hands thrown on the pillow like a drowned man.
He'd walked back through the Red Light District
and seen the beckoning girls. He'd beckoned them
to step out from the glass. 'Come and hear my news,'
he mouthed. And his mind sang. She lives, she lives.

BLACK

One day, the girl who usually wore colours,
fierce reds, sea-greens and -blues, butter yellows,
was wearing black. I made some passing comment -
"you'll doom the week" or "why so like a crow?" -
before I realised what I'd done. This was the one,
I'd heard them whispering, who'd had bad news from home.

Next time we met, I cried, suddenly knowing
what it was to have a sister who had died
and then to have some crass idiot cracking jokes.
But she, as if it eased her grief to comfort mine,
told me not to blame my tongue. I looked again.
Black was a radiance, its nimbus pity, its centre pain.

A HUNT IN THE DARK FOREST

- a painting by Paolo Uccello,
        in the Ashmolean Museum, Oxford

Uccello wanted to paint darkness
so first of all he painted white -
the great block of horse and rider
in the right foreground, the flowers
dotted on the grass, the blossoms
in the forest crown. Then he painted red:
sashes of the knights and foot-hunters, flags,
more flowers, blossoms, horses. Then brown,
the bays and duns, the stags themselves,
running, falling, dying on the floor,
the approach of darkness but not the darkness yet.

Already he had painted green and blue,
the deepening forest, carving out a space
behind the canvas that stretched at least a mile,
a silver strand of river narrowing in a vee.
His faith was in technique. It worked.
Spear-tips. Buckles. Finally, he loosed the hounds,
white, red, brown, the same leaping form
diminishing in size as they followed blood,
until only the palest ones could be seen,
yelping and chasing in the far distance,
as close to our noses as the first.

This is how Uccello, the naive calculator,
painted darkness and never painted black -
                sending the pack
of luminous dogs hunting the furthest prey.

THE FOREST FIRE

- a painting by Piero di Cosimo,
          in the Ashmolean Museum, Oxford.

Piero di Cosimo loved freaks,
loved the mannerisms of the genes.
Out of the fire at the core of the forest,
come leaping and plunging odd mis-shaped things,
lopsided cattle with scorch-marked hides,
a flame-cowed lion, a fowl plummeting to earth,
a mother-bear with half-licked cubs,
even a pigeon made enormous by perspective,
asquat the foreground like a vernacular phoenix.

They occupy the main spaces
tongues lolling, flanks heaving, eyes bulging,
stalled at the borderline the frame creates.
Far in the distance, his brush picked out
traceries of swallows across the sky,
an arabesque of hares swimming the lake,
but where a master would have placed a goddess,
Piero puts a naked tree, charred and twisted.
A puff of fire carries copse to copse. The old wood burns.

Not everything is on the move.
Two creatures are browsing among a herd of others,
all with bulky deer-like bodies, whose prehensile lips
nibble at low-hanging branches or crop the grass.
These two alone have human faces,
                 strangely contented,
as if by a forbidden mating
they have found their animal selves.
Piero di Cosimo loves these freaks. He paints them last.

OPHELIA AND HAMLET

So prettily Ophelia floats among her flowers.
Daddy weeps. Ooooooo. Ooooooo. Ooooooo.
He put her there.
Who else told her to walk at her orisons
and catch the prince? Who taught her such pretty manners
that even in death she arches her fingers palm upwards
as if she plucked a note out of the virginal air?
It's always Daddies who make Ophelias what they are,
not the men who would have made them moon-blessed queens.

So wittily Prince Hamlet conducts his madness.
Mummy weeps. Ooooooo. Ooooooo. Ooooooo.
She put him there.
Who else told him 'I love you' with her every glance,
then stole away to Uncle's bed? Who taught him such vanity
that even insane his clothes are just-so disarranged,
a moody black that flatters the pallor of his face?
It's always Mummies that make mad princes what they are,
not the women who would have made them sun-bright kings.

SOCRATES IN THE CITY

Someone has stuffed a fag-end
up the nostril of 'Dead Socrates',
sitting slouched on the pedestal
with a clear broad thinker's brow
at the mercy of fumes and graffiti.

Leaning across him, as a friend
must have done to check the pulse
or close the lids, I take away
the sacrilegious nicotine-stump,
our drug not his, that blocks the breath.

As I do so, at first accidentally
and then with a quickening of my heart,
I grip, and feel the comfort of,
the great marble five-ridged hand.
The touch is real. Death and the city not.

from VARIATIONS ON LAWRENCE
BAXTER AND CLARA

one of a series of poems where characters from
'Sons and Lovers' are transposed to late 20th century Britain

Baxter glowered. Clara stood her ground and scorned him,
one of the quarrels that wrecked their early days of love.
Perhaps if there'd been kids… If her mother hadn't interfered…
If she'd controlled her temper and he'd controlled the drink.
Through the open windows, their voices sounded, hers stronger,
like a lance. He punched her chest. She kneed him in the groin.
Police found them, her cheek-flap loose, blouse ripped to her bra,
on his back like a cat, clawing any soft part. Separating them
cost a torn eye and a torn uniform. The end of marriage.

Charged with assault, sacked the next day, Baxter disappeared.
She knew that he had family in the north, his gypsy uncles
who traded horses on the edge of the moors. As for her,
she continued in the town, bearing the stigma like the scar
that went from hairline to jawbone. She studied Open University
but lacked the patience. The long measured words angered her,
not because she didn't understand - she'd never been daft -
but because they seemed to deny the language of passion
which spoke in her veins and made her miss the blundering fool

She dreamed of him, drowned in the water of a black brook.
In fact, he huddled by a factory vent for warmth, ragged
along with hopeless others, different stories ending the same.
That winter nearly killed him. Down south, she met a woman
who told her in a pub, 'It's easy money.'
                        Out on the London Road, she pushed sex
to hypocrites in cruising cars, lawyers, dons, consultants,
seeking one of the hardened women, mini-skirted in the frost
that stiffened all the trees on the common. Her temper flared.
By spring, she took up studying again. He was coughing blood.

A bearded priest befriended him. Laundering his clothes,
he found a photo from a booth, staring eyes, wild heavy hair,

an address in smudged ballpoint, dating from their courtship.
Months later, when Baxter's health was sound and the summer
coursing in his limbs, the priest wrote to arrange a meeting.
In a neutral place, a large town. They travelled there by train
through midland countryside, the trees russet, cattle grazing.
Near Nottingham, Baxter panicked. Clara felt for the first time
the shame of what she'd done. Neither got out. Their trains passed.

The degree seemed easy after that. What was all the fuss about,
the robes, the congratulations, people treating her as special?
It helped her put the past aside, no longer seeing in every man
one of her clients at the kerb. Baxter was learning new skills,
his broad fingers tapping a keyboard.
                    He'd learnt to sacrifice male pride,
not as clumsy as he'd thought. Within months, he had a job,
a VDU operator. He met and partnered a sparrow-boned blonde,
taking on her five children, fighting the bastard who'd left her
but come back when he'd heard she had a man. Clara went abroad.

In the Louvre, she wrote her thesis, about pre-Roman art,
countering the old dogma of Lawrence in Etruscan Places,
but felt a kinship with his passion, seeing the terracotta pair
of tomb statues, perhaps a king and queen, perhaps mythical,
smiling through time at each other, reclining side by side.
She sent a postcard of them to the last address she knew.
It arrived in May. The woman at his shoulder said, "Who's 'C'?"
Then he went to bath the kids while she was cooking dinner.
He threw the card in pieces into the river. She got her Ph.D.

For him, an early heart attack. An undetected cancer did for her.
In both cases, their friends said they'd had a life well-lived,
brought happiness to family and neighbours, colleagues, others.
"Nobody asks much more than that." Laid out on a slab, nude,
as they had been in bed together in one cherry-blossom May,
they'd have made a brawny well-matched couple, the little
differences of sex - her heavy pubic bush and fleshy breasts,
his paunch and pale testicles - insignificant beside their sameness,
as if they'd have been better born sister and brother.
                    Then love would have been good.

THE BREAD OF HEAVEN TREE

Under the flowering tree, he'd sat and read
all afternoon, Hardy, his favourite over
sixty years, Tess and Jude re-read until
they must have seemed the bedrock of his life:
two marriages, two wars, three sons who all
betrayed him, so he thought, spending their time
in widow-courting, drunkenness, silence abroad.

Checking as it grew dark, I found him slumped -
a heart attack - his face hidden in his lap,
as if he shunned the light. Pigeons whirlpooled,
with a rush of wingbeats like a haywire clock,
and loaves of yeastily-scented blossom veered
on the breeze when I came to lift his head
from the dour pages sprinkled with heaven's bread.

CREDO

How can 'I' stay in touch with 'you'? Confidently,
The stars above you/Know I love you, sings the radio.
But 'you' is a promiscuous, flirty word. An easy rhyme.
Don't trust it. Trust myself instead, the 'I' in time.

Yet if each neural pulse creates a new persona,
the next one faithless to the last, where's the guarantee
that, when time flicks its tail, I'll recognise 'me'?

Alarm-clock-early though, I get your call. So what?
All I have is the frail substance of a faceless voice,
a fabrication of the wires, coded and de-coded, noise.

But then we chatter - joking - and, at the just moment,
say together, our tongues marrying and chiming true,
for the first time, fleeting and for ever: "I LOVE YOU."

The three syllables spiral in our ears - Matisse's
dancers linking hands or Keats's revellers on the urn -
a molecule of verbal matter which nobody can prise apart.
How do we know if what we touch stays true?
                                        Trust life. Trust art